FINANCE FOR STUDENTS:
THE FOUNDATION FOR FINANCIAL FREEDOM

Sola E. Akinola

FINANCE FOR STUDENTS: THE FOUNDATION FOR FINANCIAL FREEDOM
© Copyright 2023 SOLA E. AKINOLA

Published in
Nigeria by:
Nkanemi Services
nkanemiservices@gmail.com

All rights reserved. No portion of this book may be reproduced, stored in a retrieval system, or transmitted in any form or by any means without the prior written permission of the author except for brief quotations in critical reviews or articles.

CONTENT

Chapter I. Introduction
   A. Financial Stages in Life
   B. Importance of financial education for students

Chapter II. Understanding Personal Finance
   A. Budgeting and managing expenses
   B. Saving and investing for the future
   C. Importance of setting financial goals

Chapter III. Building a Strong Financial Foundation
   A. Understanding student loans and managing debt
   B. Establishing and managing credit
   C. Building an emergency fund

Chapter IV. Investing Basics for Students
   A. Introduction to different investment options
   B. Risk and reward considerations for young investors
   C. Long-term vs. short-term investment strategies

Chapter V. Smart Money Habits and Strategies
   A. Making wise financial decisions as a student
   B. Strategies for saving and investing on a limited budget
   C. Understanding the power of compound interest

Chapter VI. Planning for the Future
   A. Introduction to retirement planning for students
   B. Exploring various retirement savings options
   C. Creating a financial roadmap for life after graduation

Chapter VII. Navigating Financial Challenges
    A. Dealing with unexpected financial setbacks
    B. Strategies for managing financial stress as a student
    C. Seeking professional financial advice when needed

Chapter VIII. Real-Life Case Studies
    A. Success stories of students who achieved financial freedom
    B. Learning from the experiences of others

Chapter IX. Tools and Resources
    A. Recommended financial apps and tools for students
    B. Useful websites and books for further learning

Chapter X. Practical Strategies to achieve Financial Freedom

Chapter XI. Conclusion

Chapter I
INTRODUCTION

Welcome to "Finance for Students: The Foundation for Financial Freedom." In this comprehensive guide, I embark on a journey to empower you with the knowledge and tools to navigate the world of personal finance successfully. As a student, you stand at the precipice of a bright future, and understanding the principles of finance is the key to unlocking a world of opportunities and achieving financial freedom.

This book is specifically designed for students like you, recognizing the unique challenges and opportunities you face during your educational journey. Whether you are a high school student seeking for productive ventures, a university student navigating the complexities of managing your allowance, seeking opportunities for more income to survive, loans from friends or family, or a recent graduate stepping into the workforce, this book has something valuable to offer.

My plan is clear, straight forward and simple but yet powerful: to provide you with a strong foundation in financial literacy, enabling you to make informed decisions about your money and set yourself on a path to financial independence. Through practical advice, real-life case studies, and accessible explanations, we will explore budgeting, saving, investing, and more, tailored to your needs as a student.

As you turn the pages of this book, you will learn how to avoid common financial pitfalls, build a secure financial future, and develop the mindset and habits essential for achieving long-term financial success. It's time to take charge of your finances, and with the right knowledge and determination, you can shape a prosperous and fulfilling future.

So, let's embark on this empowering journey together. Embrace the opportunities ahead, and let "Finance for Students: The Foundation for Financial Freedom" be your guiding light towards a lifetime of financial well-being. Let's get started!

Finance is the discipline that deals with the management, allocation, and study of money, assets, investments, and liabilities. It encompasses various activities related to the acquisition and utilization of funds by individuals, businesses, governments, and other entities.

In the context of personal finance, it involves managing your own money, making decisions about budgeting, saving, investing, and handling debt. On a broader scale, corporate finance focuses on financial management and decision-making within companies, including capital budgeting, financial analysis, and risk management.

Public finance deals with the management of funds by governments and public institutions, including taxation, budgeting, and public spending. International finance, on the other hand, involves financial transactions and interactions between different countries and their currencies.

The overall goal of finance is to optimize the allocation of resources, manage risks, and maximize the value of investments. It plays a crucial role in the functioning of economies, businesses, and individuals, influencing economic growth and stability at various levels.

The term "finance for students" refers to the specific area of financial education and management that is targeted towards students. It involves teaching and providing resources to help students understand various aspects of personal finance, money management, and financial planning.

Finance for students covers a wide range of topics, including budgeting, saving, investing, managing debt, understanding credit, and making informed financial decisions. The goal is to equip students with the knowledge and skills they need to handle their finances responsibly during their student years and beyond.

Financial education for students is essential because it lays the groundwork for building strong financial foundations, fostering responsible money habits, and preparing them for the financial challenges they may encounter throughout their lives. By understanding finance, students can make informed choices about their spending, saving, and investing, leading to a more financially secure future.

The term "finance for students" refers to the domain of financial education and management that specifically caters to students' needs and circumstances. It encompasses the knowledge, skills, and practices related to personal finance that are relevant and applicable to students during their academic years and beyond.

Finance for students includes various aspects such as understanding budgeting, managing expenses, saving, investing, handling student loans, building credit, and making informed financial decisions. The primary objective is to empower students with the necessary financial literacy and tools to manage their money effectively and responsibly.

By learning about finance for students, young individuals can develop the financial acumen necessary to navigate the financial challenges they may encounter during their educational journey and prepare themselves for a stable and successful financial future. It equips them with the knowledge to establish a strong financial foundation, make prudent financial choices, and work towards achieving financial freedom and security throughout their lives.

Finance for students is critical and serve as a foundation for financial freedom. This suggests that gaining knowledge and understanding of personal finance during one's student years serves as the groundwork for achieving long-term financial independence and security.

When students acquire essential financial skills, such as budgeting, saving, investing, and debt management, they establish a strong financial foundation. This knowledge empowers them to make informed decisions about their money, avoid common financial pitfalls, and cultivate responsible financial habits early in life.

By building a solid financial foundation during their student years, individuals can set themselves on a path towards achieving financial freedom in the future. They are better equipped to handle financial challenges, such as student loans, credit management, and unexpected expenses, while also positioning themselves to capitalize on opportunities for financial growth and stability.

In a nutshell, finance for students as a foundation for financial freedom emphasizes the importance of starting early and using the student years as a platform to gain the necessary financial literacy and skills to create a prosperous and financially secure future. It encourages students to take charge of their finances, make wise money decisions, and work towards attaining financial independence and freedom throughout their lives.

A. Financial Stages in Life

Financial stages in life refer to the different phases that individuals typically go through in their financial journey. These stages can vary depending on personal circumstances, but generally, they can be classified as follows:

Early adulthood:
Starting out in the workforce or pursuing higher education.
Establishing financial independence from parents or guardians.
Learning to manage basic financial responsibilities, such as budgeting and saving.

Young professionals:
Advancing in one's career and earning a more substantial income.
Accumulating debt from student loans or other financial obligations.
Focusing on building an emergency fund and paying off debts.

Family formation:
Getting married or starting a long-term committed relationship.
Purchasing a home or considering homeownership.
Planning for and managing the financial responsibilities of raising a family.

Mid-career and peak earning years:
Earning a higher income as one gain experience and expertise in their career.
Contributing more towards retirement accounts and long-term investments.

Balancing financial priorities between family needs and saving for the future.

Pre-retirement:
Approaching retirement age and assessing retirement readiness.
Adjusting investment strategies to minimize risk while preserving wealth.
Creating a comprehensive retirement plan and estimating retirement income needs.

Retirement:
Transitioning from work life to a period of financial independence.
Managing investments to generate income while ensuring funds last throughout retirement.
Exploring options for Social Security benefits and pension distributions.

Future life:
Addressing potential healthcare and long-term care costs.
Making estate planning arrangements to pass on assets to beneficiaries.
Navigating financial decisions related to senior living arrangements.

It's important to note that these financial stages are not fixed, and individuals may experience them differently based on various factors such as career choices, financial decisions, economic conditions, and life events. Additionally, some people may experience more or fewer stages depending on their unique circumstances. The key is to be proactive in managing finances and planning for the future at each stage of life.

Ultimately, there are three strategical approaches to accomplish your life financial freedom:

1. Get a high paying job, a raise at your income or that of any member of the family that can support your dream.
2. Earn money on the side with skills you already have. That is, the need to create side hustle.
3. Lunch your own business. This is very crucial because it is more enduring and sustainable both in the short and long run.

B. Importance of Financial Education for Students

Financial education for students is of paramount importance for several reasons:

1. Building Strong Financial Foundations: Financial education will equip you with essential knowledge and skills to manage money effectively. It will help you to develop responsible financial habits early in life, leading to a solid financial foundation for your future.

2. Making Informed Financial Decisions: With financial education, you can make informed decisions about spending, saving, and investing. You will learn to evaluate financial options critically and understand the consequences of your choices.

3. Avoiding Debt Traps: Understanding the risks of debt and learning how to manage it can prevent you from falling into

unnecessary and excessive debt or credit card traps that can lead to financial stress and burdensome obligations.

4. Developing Financial Literacy: Financial education will increase your financial literacy, allowing you to understand financial concepts, terms, and products, empowering you to navigate the complex financial landscape confidently.

5. Fostering Financial Responsibility: By learning about budgeting, setting financial goals, and saving, you will become more responsible and accountable for your financial decisions and actions.

6. Preparing for the Future: Financial education will prepare you for life after school, enabling you to handle financial challenges, such as paying off debts, student loans, finding affordable housing, and planning for retirement.

7. Cultivating Financial Confidence: Knowledge of personal finance will build your level of confidence to manage your financial affairs independently and avoid being vulnerable to financial scams or misinformation.

8. Reducing Stress and Anxiety: Financial education can reduce stress and anxiety related to money matters by providing you with practical tools and strategies to handle financial difficulties proactively.

9. Empowering Economic Citizenship: As a financially educated student, you become active participant in the economy,

contributing to financial stability and growth on both personal and societal levels.

10. Breaking Cycles of Poverty: Financial education can play a crucial role in breaking the cycle of poverty by empowering you with the knowledge and skills to make better financial choices, leading to greater economic mobility.

In a nutshell, financial education is an investment in the future well-being, empowering you to take control of your finances, achieve your goals, and work towards financial freedom and security.

Chapter II
UNDERSTANDING PERSONAL FINANCE

Understanding Personal Finance refers to the knowledge and comprehension of managing your personal finances effectively. It involves the ability to make informed and responsible decisions about money matters that directly impact your financial well-being.

Key components of understanding personal finance include:

1. Budgeting: Creating and maintaining a budget that outlines income, expenses, and financial goals, allowing you to allocate your money wisely and prioritize your spending.

2. Saving: Learning to set aside a portion of income for future needs and emergencies, fostering financial stability and providing a safety net during unforeseen circumstances.

3. Investing: Understanding different investment options, such as stocks, bonds, mutual funds, and real estate, and making informed decisions to grow wealth over time.

4. Managing Debt: Developing strategies to manage and reduce debt responsibly, including credit card debt, student loans, mortgages, and other debts.

5. Credit Management: Learning about credit scores, credit reports, and building a positive credit history to access favorable financial opportunities and interest rates.

6. Financial Goal Setting: Establishing clear and achievable financial objectives, such as saving for retirement, purchasing a home, or funding education.

7. Risk Management: Understanding and acquiring appropriate insurance coverage to protect against financial risks and uncertainties.

8. Financial Literacy: Acquiring knowledge of financial concepts, terminology, and financial products to make informed decisions and avoid financial pitfalls.

Understanding Personal Finance is essential for you to gain control over your financial lives, make wise financial decisions, and work towards achieving financial security, independence, and long-term prosperity.

A. Budgeting and managing expenses.

Budgeting and managing expenses are crucial aspects of personal finance that involve planning, tracking, and controlling your financial resources effectively. These are the breakdown of each component:

1. Budgeting:
Budgeting is the process of creating a detailed plan for how to allocate and manage income to cover expenses, savings, and financial goals. It involves analyzing and categorizing income sources and expenditures to ensure that spending aligns with financial priorities. A budget typically includes:

   - Income: All sources of money coming in, such as your allowance, gifts from family or friend, money from side hustle, bonuses, or other earnings.

- Expenses: A breakdown of all the necessary and discretionary expenses, such as school fees, house rent, utilities, groceries, transportation, entertainment, and other recurring costs.
- Savings: Allocation of money towards savings accounts or investment vehicles for future financial goals.
- Emergency Fund: Setting aside funds to cover unexpected expenses or emergencies.
- Financial Goals: Allocating funds towards specific financial objectives, like paying off debt, personal growth or funding professional education or certification.

2. Managing Expenses:
Managing expenses involves controlling spending to ensure that it aligns with your budget and financial goals. Effective expense management include the following:

- Prioritization: Identifying essential expenses that must be covered first before allocating funds to discretionary spending.
- Tracking: Keeping records of all expenditures to monitor spending patterns and identify areas where adjustments are needed.
- Cutting Unnecessary Costs: Identifying and eliminating non-essential expenses to free up funds for more critical financial priorities.
- Avoiding Debt: Managing expenses to avoid accumulating excessive debt and ensuring debt payments fit within the budget.
- Reviewing and Adjusting: Periodically reviewing the budget, assessing progress towards financial goals, and making adjustments as necessary based on changes in income or expenses.

Budgeting and managing expenses are essential practices for maintaining financial stability and achieving financial objectives. By creating a realistic budget and effectively managing spending, you can gain control over your finances, reduce financial stress, and work towards building a secure financial future.

B. Saving and investing for the future

Saving and investing for the future are two interconnected financial practices that involve setting aside money to build wealth and achieve long-term financial goals. Let's explore each concept:

1. Saving:
Saving refers to the act of setting aside a portion of your income for future use rather than spending it immediately. The primary purpose of saving is to accumulate funds for short-term goals or emergencies. Key aspects of saving include:

   - Emergency Fund: Building a savings buffer to cover unexpected expenses or emergencies, providing financial security and peace of mind.
   - Short-Term Goals: Saving for specific expenses that are anticipated in the near future, such as travelling for a program or a vacation, purchasing of books, or down payment for items like computer.
   - Regular Contributions: Consistently adding money to a savings account or other safe, easily accessible financial instruments.

2. Investing:
Investing involves putting money into various financial assets or instruments with the expectation of generating a return over time. Unlike saving, which usually aims to keep you going as a sustainable strategy, investing aims to grow wealth for the future. Key aspects of investing include:

  - Long-Term Goals: Investing for future financial objectives that might be several years or decades away, such as funding for life after school, marriage, children's education or retirement.

  - Risk and Return: Understanding that different investment options carry varying levels of risk and potential return, and aligning investments with your risk tolerance and financial goals.

  - Diversification: Spreading investments across different asset classes, sectors, or geographic regions to reduce risk and increase the potential for growth.

  - Compound Growth: This strategy is very critical at this stage that is taking advantage of the power of compound interest, where earnings on investments can generate additional earnings over time.

Saving and investing complement each other in financial planning. While saving helps create a financial safety net and meet short-term goals, investing enables you to achieve long-term financial objectives and build wealth over time. Balancing both practices is essential for securing financial stability and maximizing the potential for long-term financial success.

C. Importance of setting financial goals

Setting financial goals is crucial for several reasons as it plays a significant role in personal finance and long-term financial success. These are some key reasons highlighting the importance of setting financial goals:

1. Focus and Clarity: Financial goals provide a clear direction and focus for managing money and making financial decisions. They give you a purpose for your financial actions, making it easier to prioritize and align spending, saving, and investing with your objectives.

2. Motivation and Discipline: Having specific financial goals will motivate you to stay disciplined and committed to your financial plans. It will help you to resist impulsive spending and make choices that align with your long-term objectives.

3. Measure Progress: Financial goals serve as benchmarks to measure progress and success. Regularly tracking progress towards achieving these goals provides a sense of accomplishment and keeps you on track to achieve your desired financial outcomes.

4. Financial Planning: Setting goals is an essential part of financial planning. It allows you to map out the steps needed to achieve your objectives, identify potential obstacles, and create a realistic roadmap for your financial journey.

5. Financial Security: Financial goals help create a safety net and build financial resilience. For example, having an emergency fund as a financial goal can provide a buffer during unexpected situations, reducing financial stress and vulnerability.

6. Long-Term Vision: Setting financial goals encourages you to think about your long-term financial future and consider how your current financial decisions will impact your lives years down the line.

7. Prioritization: Financial goals help prioritize spending and saving decisions. Financial goals enable you to allocate resources efficiently towards what truly matters to you, allowing you to balance immediate needs with long-term aspirations.

8. Empowerment: Having clear financial goals will empower you to take control of your finances. It instills a sense of ownership over your financial well-being and encourages proactive financial decision-making.

9. Retirement Planning: Setting retirement goals is essential for building a secure financial future. Having a clear retirement vision will enable you to plan and save accordingly to enjoy your golden years comfortably.

10. Realizing Dreams and Aspirations: Financial goals can be tied to personal dreams and aspirations. Whether it's traveling, buying a home in the future, or starting a business, setting financial goals will help turn these dreams into achievable realities.

In conclusion, setting financial goals is a fundamental step towards financial success and well-being. It provides purpose, direction, and discipline in managing finances, helping you to build a strong financial foundation and work towards achieving your financial aspirations.

Chapter III
BUILDING A STRONG FINANCIAL FOUNDATION

Building a Strong Financial Foundation is the process of establishing a solid and stable financial framework upon which you can build your financial well-being and achieve your long-term goals. It involves adopting responsible financial practices, making informed decisions, and creating a solid financial base that can withstand unexpected challenges and support future financial growth.

Key aspects of building a strong financial foundation include:

1. Budgeting and Saving: Creating a budget to manage income and expenses effectively, while setting aside a portion of earnings for savings and emergency funds.

2. Debt Management: Understanding and managing debts responsibly to avoid excessive financial burdens and prioritize debt repayment.

3. Financial Literacy: Gaining knowledge and understanding of financial concepts, products, and strategies to make informed financial decisions.

4. Setting Financial Goals: Identifying and prioritizing short-term and long-term financial goals to guide financial planning and decision-making.

5. Investing Wisely: Learning about investment options and aligning investments with risk tolerance and financial objectives.

6. Insurance Coverage: Ensuring appropriate insurance coverage to protect against unexpected financial losses and mitigate risks.

7. Retirement Planning: Planning and saving for retirement to secure financial stability during post-work years.

8. Building Credit: Establishing and maintaining a positive credit history to access better financial opportunities and lower interest rates.

9. Continual Review and Adjustment: Regularly assessing and adjusting financial strategies as life circumstances change or new opportunities arise.

10. Financial Discipline: Exercising discipline in financial habits and decisions to avoid impulsive spending and stay focused on long-term financial objectives.

Building a strong financial foundation is a fundamental step towards achieving financial security, independence, and freedom. It provides you with the tools and knowledge needed to navigate financial challenges, capitalize on opportunities, and work towards a prosperous financial future.

A. Understanding student loans and managing debt

Understanding student loans and managing debt is essential for students and graduates to navigate their educational expenses and financial obligations responsibly. Let's break down each aspect:

1. Understanding Student Loans:
 - Types of Student Loans: Knowing the different types of student loans available, such as federal loans, bank loans, private loans, subsidized, and unsubsidized loans.
 - Interest Rates and Terms: Understanding the interest rates, repayment terms, and grace periods associated with student loans.
 - Borrowing Limits: Being aware of the maximum loan amounts that can be borrowed each academic year and throughout the educational journey.
 - FAFSA and Financial Aid: Understanding the process of filling out the Free Application for Federal Student Aid (FAFSA) to determine eligibility for federal financial aid.

2. Managing Debt:
 - Budgeting for Repayment: Creating a budget that accounts for student loan repayment as a fixed expense and ensuring it fits within the overall financial plan.
 - Loan Repayment Options: Understanding the various loan repayment plans, such as standard, income-driven, or graduated plans, and selecting the one that aligns with your financial circumstances.
 - Timely Payments: Making timely loan payments to avoid late fees, penalties, and negative impacts on credit scores.

- Exploring Loan Forgiveness: Being aware of loan forgiveness programs and understanding the eligibility criteria and requirements.

- Avoiding Default: Knowing the consequences of loan default and seeking assistance or repayment options if experiencing financial hardship.

Understanding student loans and managing debt is very crucial for you to make informed decisions about your educational financing and to avoid potential financial pitfalls in the future. By being proactive and responsible in managing debt, you can ensure a smoother transition to post-graduation financial responsibilities and pave the way for a more secure financial future.

B. Establishing and managing credit

Understanding the approaches of establishing and managing credit is vital for individuals seeking to build a positive credit history, which plays a significant role in various financial aspects of life. Let's delve into each aspect for the details:

1. Establishing Credit:
   - Credit History: Understanding that credit history is a record of an individual's borrowing and repayment activities, including credit cards, loans, and other debts.
   - Credit Reports: Being aware of credit reports, which summarize credit history and are maintained by credit bureaus, such as CRC Credit Bureau, Equifax, Experian, and TransUnion.

- Building Credit: Knowing the ways to build credit, such as opening a credit card, becoming an authorized user on someone else's account, or taking out a small loan.

2. Managing Credit:
- Responsible Credit Card Use: Learning to use credit cards responsibly by paying bills on time and avoiding carrying high balances.
- Credit Utilization: Understanding credit utilization, which is the percentage of available credit being used, and maintaining a low utilization rate to improve credit scores.
- Regular Monitoring: Regularly checking credit reports for accuracy and identifying any errors or fraudulent activities.
- Credit Scores: Understanding credit scores, such as CRC score (Individual), FICO scores, and how they are calculated based on credit history, payment history, credit utilization, and other factors.
- Avoiding Overborrowing: Being cautious not to overextend credit and accumulate debts beyond the ability to repay.

Establishing and managing credit wisely is crucial for obtaining future loans, mortgages, and other forms of credit at favorable interest rates. A positive credit history can also impact various aspects of life, such as qualifying for rental housing, securing employment, and even obtaining insurance policies. By being informed and responsible in managing credit, you can build a strong credit profile and improve your overall financial well-being.

C. Building an emergency fund

Building an emergency fund involves setting aside a designated amount of money specifically reserved to cover unexpected and urgent financial needs or emergencies. It serves as a financial safety net and provides a sense of security during times of financial stress or uncertainty. These is what it entails:

1. Purpose: The primary purpose of an emergency fund is to be prepared for unforeseen circumstances, such as purchase of course materials, laboratory equipment, expense for project, medical emergencies, car repairs, or unexpected home repairs.

2. Fund Size: The size of an emergency fund may vary depending on your circumstances and financial goals. A common recommendation for students is to set buffer limit that is peculiar to their course of study or aim for three months' worth of living expenses.

3. Regular Contributions: Building an emergency fund requires consistent and regular contributions. You may set aside a portion of your income each month until the desired fund size is achieved.

4. Easily Accessible: The emergency fund should be kept in a highly liquid and easily accessible account, such as a savings account or a money market fund. This ensures that the funds can be readily accessed when needed.

5. Separate from Other Savings: It is crucial to keep the emergency fund separate from other savings and investments to prevent using it for non-emergencies.

6. Protection from Debt: Having an emergency fund will help you to avoid going into debt or using high-interest credit cards to cover unexpected expenses.

7. Replenishing: After using the emergency fund for an actual emergency, it is essential to replenish it as soon as possible to maintain its level of financial protection.

Building an emergency fund may be difficult as a student but building and developing this culture will give you financial peace of mind, reduces stress during challenging times, and allows you to handle unexpected situations without derailing on your long-term financial goals. It is a fundamental step towards building a strong financial foundation and safeguarding against potential financial setbacks now and in the future.

Chapter IV
INVESTING BASICS FOR STUDENTS

Investing basics for students involve understanding the fundamental principles of investing and exploring various investment options suitable for young individuals with limited financial resources. These are some key investing basics that are peculiar to students:

1. Start Early: The power of compounding makes starting early one of the most significant advantages for young investors such as students. Even small contributions can grow substantially over time.

2. Education: Educate yourself about the different types of investments, such as stocks, bonds, mutual funds, exchange-traded funds (ETFs), and real estate investment trusts (REITs).

3. Risk and Return: Learn about the relationship between risk and potential return. Generally, higher-risk investments have the potential for higher returns but also come with a higher possibility of losing money.

4. Diversification: Diversifying your investments across different asset classes and industries can help reduce risk and potentially improve overall portfolio performance.

5. Long-Term Perspective: Investing is typically a long-term endeavor. Focus on long-term financial goals, and avoid making hasty decisions based on short-term market fluctuations.

6. Investment Accounts: Consider opening tax-advantaged accounts, such as a Roth IRA or a traditional IRA, to benefit from tax benefits while saving for retirement.

7. Dollar-Cost Averaging: Invest regularly, regardless of market conditions. This strategy, known as dollar-cost averaging, helps average out the cost of investments over time.

8. Avoid High Fees: Be mindful of investment fees, as high fees can erode returns over the long term. Look for low-cost investment options.

9. Seek Professional Advice: If you're unsure about investing, consider seeking guidance from a financial advisor to help you develop a suitable investment strategy.

10. Stay Informed: Keep yourself informed about economic trends, financial news, and investment strategies to make informed decisions.

Remember that investing involves risk, and there are no guarantees of positive returns. However, by understanding the basics and following a prudent approach, as a student you can start building you investment portfolio and work towards achieving your financial goals over time.

A. Introduction to different investment options

There are several investment options available for students, each with its own risk and return characteristics. These are some common investment options that students can consider:

1. Stocks: Investing in individual company stocks will allow you to become partial owners of the company and potentially benefit from its growth and dividend payments. Stocks offer the potential for high returns but also come with higher risk.

2. Bonds: Bonds are debt securities issued by governments or corporations, and investors receive regular interest payments until the bond's maturity date. Bonds are generally considered lower-risk investments compared to stocks.

3. Mutual Funds: Mutual funds pool money from multiple investors to invest in a diversified portfolio of stocks, bonds, or other assets. They are managed by professional fund managers and provide instant diversification.

4. Exchange-Traded Funds (ETFs): Similar to mutual funds, ETFs hold a basket of assets, but they trade on stock exchanges like individual stocks. ETFs offer flexibility and diversification.

5. Real Estate Investment Trusts (REITs): REITs are companies that own, operate, or finance income-generating real estate. Investing in REITs allows students to participate in real estate ownership without directly owning property.

6. Certificate of Deposit (CD): CDs are low-risk, fixed-term deposits offered by banks with a specified interest rate. The money is locked in for a specific period, and there are penalties for early withdrawal.

7. Peer-to-Peer Lending: Students can consider peer-to-peer lending platforms where they lend money to individuals or small businesses in exchange for interest payments.

8. Retirement Accounts: Opening an Individual Retirement Account (IRA) or Roth IRA allows students to save for retirement with potential tax benefits.

9. High-Yield Savings Accounts: While not technically an investment, high-yield savings accounts offer higher interest rates than regular savings accounts and can be a good place to keep emergency funds.

10. Education Savings Accounts: Students can save for education expenses, such as college tuition, using tax-advantaged accounts like 529 plans or Coverdell Education Savings Accounts (ESA).

It's essential for you to consider your risk appetite and tolerance, financial goals, and investment horizon when choosing among these options. Diversifying across different asset classes can help manage risk and potentially improve overall investment performance. Before making any investment decisions, it's advisable to conduct research and, if necessary, seek guidance from a financial advisor.

B. Risk and reward considerations for young investors

Risk and reward considerations are crucial for students as young investors as they navigate the world of investing. Understanding the relationship between risk and potential return is essential for making informed investment decisions. These are the breakdown of these considerations:

1. Risk:
   - Market Risk: All investments carry market risk, which is the possibility that the value of an investment may fluctuate due to changes in the overall market conditions, economic factors, or investor sentiment.
   - Volatility: Some investments, such as stocks, can experience significant price fluctuations in the short term, leading to increased volatility and potential for loss.
   - Time Horizon: Young investors have a longer time horizon, which may allow them to take on more risk since they have more time to recover from market downturns.
   - Risk Tolerance: Understanding personal risk tolerance is crucial. Some investors may be comfortable with higher risk for potentially higher returns, while others prefer more conservative investments.

2. Reward:
   - Return Potential: Higher-risk investments, such as stocks, have the potential for higher returns over the long term. Conversely, lower-risk investments like bonds may offer more modest returns.

- Compound Growth: Young investors can benefit from the power of compounding, where investment earnings generate additional earnings over time, leading to exponential growth.

3. Diversification:
   - Diversification is a strategy that involves spreading investments across different asset classes, industries, or regions. It helps reduce risk by not putting all eggs in one basket and may improve overall portfolio performance.

4. Investment Goals:
   - Young investors should align their risk and reward considerations with their investment goals. Short-term goals may require more stable investments, while long-term goals may accommodate higher-risk investments.

5. Educate and Research:
   - Being well-informed about different investments and conducting thorough research is essential for young investors to make informed decisions that match their risk tolerance and financial objectives.

6. Review and Adjust:
   - Regularly review investment portfolios and adjust the allocation as needed based on changes in risk tolerance, investment goals, and market conditions.

Students as young investors should strike a balance between risk and reward that aligns with their individual financial situation and long-term goals. By understanding these considerations and taking a prudent approach to investing, you can work towards building a successful investment strategy that sets you on a path towards financial prosperity.

C. Long-term vs. short-term investment strategies

Long-term and short-term investment strategies are two distinct approaches that you can consider based on your financial goals, risk tolerance, and time horizon. Let us do a quick comparison of these strategies:

Long-Term Investment Strategy:
1. Time Horizon: Long-term investments are typically held for several years or even decades. Students with long-term financial goals, such as buying a car, building a house, making down payment for mortgage, retirement or funding education for their children, can benefit from this approach.
2. Risk Tolerance: Long-term investments often involve higher-risk assets, such as stocks, as they have the potential for higher returns over extended periods. Students with a higher risk tolerance may find long-term strategies suitable.
3. Compounding: This is a great opportunity for Students. The power of compounding is a significant advantage for long-term investors. Reinvesting earnings over time can lead to exponential growth in investment value.
4. Patience: Long-term strategies require patience and discipline, as they may experience short-term market fluctuations.
5. Diversification: Diversifying across different asset classes is essential to reduce risk in a long-term portfolio.

Short-Term Investment Strategy:
1. Time Horizon: Short-term investments are held for a shorter period, typically less than a year. Students with immediate financial needs, such as funding for a project study, a semester abroad or making a down payment on a car, may opt for short-term strategies.
2. Risk Tolerance: Short-term investments tend to be more conservative, focusing on low-risk assets like bonds or money market funds, to protect principal and ensure liquidity.
3. Liquidity: Short-term investments prioritize liquidity, allowing quick access to funds when needed.
4. Preservation of Capital: The primary goal of short-term strategies is to preserve capital rather than seek significant growth.
5. Flexibility: Short-term investments offer flexibility, as students may need to liquidate them at any time without incurring substantial losses.

Combining Both Strategies:
You can strike a balance between long-term and short-term investment strategies. For example, you can invest a portion of your funds in long-term assets for future goals like retirement and another portion in short-term assets to cover immediate expenses or emergencies. This hybrid approach will allow you to take advantage of both growth potential and liquidity.

Ultimately, the choice of investment strategy depends on individual financial goals, risk tolerance, and time horizon. You should conduct thorough research, seek guidance from financial advisors if necessary, and make well-informed decisions that align with your unique circumstances and aspirations.

V. SMART MONEY HABITS AND STRATEGIES

Smart money habits and strategies are essential for you to build a strong financial foundation and set yourself up for long-term financial success. These are some key smart money habits and strategies for you to build, develop and adopt:

1. Create a Budget: Establish a budget to track income and expenses. Identify areas where spending can be reduced and allocate money wisely towards essential needs, savings, and financial goals.

2. Save Regularly: Cultivate a habit of saving money regularly, even if it's a small amount. Set up automatic transfers to savings accounts to ensure consistent contributions.

3. Build an Emergency Fund: Create an emergency fund to cover unexpected expenses or emergencies. Aim to save at least three to six months' worth of living expenses.

4. Manage Student Loans Wisely: If you have student loans, understand the terms, interest rates, and repayment options. Make timely payments and consider additional payments, when possible, to reduce the overall interest burden.

5. Use Credit Responsibly: If you have a credit card, use it responsibly and pay the balance in full each month to avoid accruing high-interest debt.

6. Invest for the Future: Start investing early, even with small amounts, to take advantage of compound growth and build wealth over time. Understand the risk and return characteristics of different investment options.

7. Practice Delayed Gratification: Avoid impulsive spending and practice delayed gratification. Consider the long-term benefits of saving and investing versus immediate consumption.

8. Prioritize Financial Goals: Set clear financial goals and prioritize them. Whether it's paying off debt, saving for a trip, or building an investment portfolio, stay focused on achieving your objectives.

9. Take Advantage of Student Discounts: As a student, look for discounts and deals that can help you save money on everyday expenses and entertainment.

10. Limit Unnecessary Expenses: Cut back on non-essential expenses, such as dining out frequently or expensive entertainment, to free up funds for more critical financial goals.

11. Seek Financial Education: Continuously educate yourself about personal finance, investing, and money management. Attend workshops, read books, and follow reputable financial blogs to expand your financial knowledge.

12. Avoid Peer Pressure Spending: Don't succumb to peer pressure when it comes to spending beyond your means. Stick to

your budget and financial goals, even if it means saying no to certain activities or purchases.

By adopting these smart money habits and strategies, you can lay a solid financial groundwork, develop responsible financial habits, and set yourself up for a financially secure and prosperous future.

A. Making wise financial decisions as a student

Making wise financial decisions as a student involves being informed, responsible, and intentional with money management. It requires understanding the consequences of financial choices and aligning them with long-term financial goals. These are the crucial understanding of making wise financial decisions:

1. Financial Literacy: Being financially literate means having the knowledge and understanding of financial concepts, budgeting, saving, investing, debt management, and other essential money-related topics.

2. Budgeting: Creating and sticking to a budget is crucial. Knowing how much money is coming in and going out helps make informed spending decisions and avoid overspending.

3. Differentiating Wants and Needs: Distinguishing between wants and needs is essential to prioritize essential expenses and avoid unnecessary spending.

4. Saving and Investing: Building the habit of saving money regularly and considering investments that align with financial goals and risk tolerance.

5. Avoiding Debt Traps: Being cautious with borrowing money, credit cards and loans to avoid excessive debt and high-interest payments. Only borrowing what can be comfortably repaid.

6. Research and Comparison: Conducting thorough research and comparing prices before making significant purchases can save money.

7. Setting Financial Goals: Establishing clear financial goals helps guide financial decisions and motivates disciplined saving and investing.

8. Seeking Advice: Seeking guidance from financial advisors or mentors can provide valuable insights and help navigate complex financial matters.

9. Living Within Means: Avoiding lifestyle inflation and living within one's means, especially during student years when income might be limited.

10. Thinking Long-Term: Considering the long-term impact of financial decisions is vital. Sometimes sacrificing short-term indulgences can lead to more significant benefits in the future.

11. Being Resilient: Understanding that financial setbacks and challenges can happen but being prepared to bounce back and learn from experiences.

12. Avoiding Impulse Buying: Taking time to think through purchases and avoiding impulsive spending can lead to better financial decisions.

Making wise financial decisions as a student lays the groundwork for a lifetime of responsible money management. By being financially aware, disciplined, and goal-oriented, you can set yourself up for a stable and prosperous financial future.

B. Strategies for saving and investing on a limited budget

Saving and investing on a limited budget can still be achievable for students with careful planning and disciplined financial practices. These are some strategies that students can adopt:

1. Start Small: Begin by saving and investing small amounts regularly, even if it's just a few naira or dollars each week or month. Over time, these small contributions can grow through compound interest.

2. Set Specific Goals: Define clear financial goals, whether it's building an emergency fund, funding a trip, or starting an investment portfolio. Having specific goals provides motivation and direction.

3. Create a Budget: Establish a budget to track income and expenses. Identify areas where expenses can be reduced to free up more money for saving and investing.

4. Prioritize Saving: Treat saving as a non-negotiable expense. Allocate a portion of income to savings before considering discretionary spending.

5. Embrace Technology: Utilize budgeting apps and investment platforms that offer automated saving and investment features. These tools can help make saving and investing seamless.

6. Take Advantage of Student Discounts: Look for discounts and deals specifically available to students to save money on everyday expenses and activities.

7. Cut Non-Essential Expenses: Identify and cut back on non-essential expenses, such as dining out frequently, entertainment subscriptions, or impulse purchases.

8. Utilize High-Yield Savings Accounts: Consider using high-yield savings accounts to earn higher interest on savings compared to traditional savings accounts.

9. Explore Low-Cost Investment Options: Look for low-cost investment vehicles like index funds or exchange-traded funds (ETFs) that offer diversified investment exposure without high fees.

10. Seek Free or Low-Cost Financial Education: Take advantage of free resources, workshops, or webinars to improve financial literacy and make informed investment decisions.

11. Save Windfalls: Whenever receiving unexpected money, such as gifts or tax refunds, consider saving a portion or using it to start investing.

12. Emphasize Long-Term Perspective: Remember that even small contributions to long-term investments can lead to substantial growth over time, thanks to compounding.

By adopting these strategies and being consistent with saving and investing efforts, you can build a solid financial foundation and set yourself up for financial success despite having a limited budget. It's crucial to be patient, stay disciplined, and make prudent financial decisions that align with long-term goals.

C. Understanding the power of compound interest

Understanding the power of compound interest is crucial for students as it demonstrates the potential for exponential growth in investments over time. Compound interest is the process of earning interest not only on the initial investment (principal) but also on the accumulated interest from previous periods. This is how it works:

1. Compound Interest on Savings: When you deposit money into a savings account, the bank pays you interest on the initial amount. In the next interest period, the interest earned in the first

period is added to the principal, and interest is then calculated on the new total. This process continues with each interest period.

2. Compound Interest on Investments: In the context of investments, compound interest applies to returns earned on investment assets. The earnings generated from investments are reinvested, leading to further growth and potential for greater returns over time.

The power of compound interest has a compounding effect, which means that the rate of growth accelerates as the investment period extends. Over longer periods, even small regular contributions can lead to substantial growth due to the cumulative effect of compounding.

For example, consider two individuals who start investing the same amount of money but for different time periods. The individual who invests for a longer duration will likely end up with significantly more wealth due to the power of compound interest.

As a student, understanding the power of compound interest emphasizes the importance of starting to save and invest early. By initiating savings and investments at a young age, you can take advantage of compounding to build substantial wealth over time, potentially setting yourself up for a financially secure future. It highlights the value of long-term investing and reinforces the benefits of disciplined saving and investing practices.

Chapter VI
PLANNING FOR THE FUTURE

Planning for the future as a student involves taking a proactive approach to set and work towards long-term goals, both academically and financially. It encompasses various aspects that contribute to personal and professional growth. This is the understanding of planning for the future as a student:

1. Academic Goals: Planning for the future academically involves setting specific objectives related to education and career aspirations. It includes choosing a field of study, identifying academic milestones, and working towards achieving good academic performance.

2. Career Exploration: You should explore potential career paths, research job opportunities, and consider internships or part-time work related to your interests. This helps in gaining practical experience and clarifying career goals.

3. Financial Planning: Planning for the future financially entails creating a budget, saving money, and investing wisely. You can start building an emergency fund and consider long-term investment strategies to secure your financial well-being.

4. Setting Personal Goals: In addition to academic and financial goals, you can set personal goals related to personal growth, health, relationships, and hobbies. Balancing personal and academic pursuits leads to a fulfilling life.

5. Networking and Building Relationships: Establishing connections with peers, professors, and professionals in the chosen field can open doors to future opportunities and support personal and professional growth.

6. Seeking Mentorship: Seeking guidance from mentors or advisors helps in making informed decisions and gaining valuable insights from experienced individuals.

7. Time Management: Developing effective time management skills will enable you to balance academic responsibilities, extracurricular activities, and personal commitments.

8. Adaptability and Flexibility: Embracing change and being adaptable to new situations enhances resilience and prepares you for future challenges.

9. Emphasizing Learning and Growth: Focus on continuous learning and personal growth by seeking out new experiences, attending workshops, or pursuing online courses.

10. Mindfulness of Well-being: Prioritizing mental and physical health is essential for maintaining overall well-being and ensuring the ability to thrive in the future.

11. Long-Term Vision: Planning for the future as a student involves considering long-term aspirations and creating a roadmap to achieve those goals over time.

By understanding the importance of planning for the future, you can make intentional decisions and take actions that align with your goals, ensuring a purposeful and successful journey towards your desired future outcomes.

A. Introduction to retirement planning for students

Retirement planning may seem distant for students, but it is never too early to start thinking about securing your financial future. As you embark on your educational journey, understanding the basics of retirement planning can set you on a path to build a comfortable and financially secure retirement.

Retirement planning involves preparing and saving for the time when you will no longer be working full-time and will depend on accumulated savings, investments, and pension plans to support your lifestyle. While retirement may seem far away, the power of compounding makes early planning highly advantageous.

In this introductory guide to retirement planning for students, we will cover essential concepts, such as:

1. The Importance of Starting Early: Discover the significant benefits of beginning your retirement planning journey during your student years and how even small contributions can lead to significant growth over time.

2. Retirement Account Options: Explore various retirement account options, such as Individual Retirement Accounts (IRAs)

and employer-sponsored retirement plans like 401(k)s, and understand the tax advantages and contribution limits of each.

3. Understanding Investment Strategies: Learn about different investment strategies that align with your risk tolerance and financial goals, helping you maximize returns while managing risk.

4. Setting Retirement Goals: Establish clear retirement goals and understand how factors like lifestyle expectations, healthcare, and inflation can impact your retirement needs.

5. The Role of Employers: Discover how employer-sponsored retirement plans can boost your retirement savings through employer matching contributions and other benefits.

6. Handling Financial Challenges: Learn how to navigate potential financial challenges during your career, such as student loan debt, while staying committed to your retirement objectives.

7. Retirement Planning Tools and Resources: Explore helpful tools and resources available for retirement planning, including retirement calculators, investment guides, and educational materials.

By developing a foundational understanding of retirement planning as a student, you can take proactive steps to secure your financial future and enjoy a comfortable retirement. Remember that every little bit of planning and saving counts, and the earlier you start, the more time you have to achieve your retirement goals. Let's embark on this journey together and set you on the path to a financially prosperous retirement.

B. Exploring various retirement savings options

As a student, you may not have a full-time income or be at the stage of your career where retirement seems like a priority. However, there are still several retirement savings options available for students to consider now or for future purposes. These are some retirement savings options that are suitable for consideration:

1. Contributory pension system

The contributory pension system is mandatory for private and public sector employees. Basically, you are the owner of a Pension Savings Account (PSA) under this scheme. In addition, a fixed amount of 15-20% of your monthly salary is deposited into this account, and insurance premiums are paid automatically. RSAs are very similar to regular savings accounts in that they both save money, but with RSAs, the fund manager invests and grows the money. In the long run, it protects your pension from inflation. You can learn more about PenCom, the organization responsible for the contributory pension scheme in Nigeria.

2. Voluntary contributions system

In addition to the contributions deducted from your account to the RSA, you can choose to contribute an additional amount. These are called voluntary contribution plans and are much more flexible than RSA fixed rates. By default, you can choose to contribute monthly, weekly, quarterly, or semi-annually. All you have to do is tell your employer and they will take care of the rest.

3. Micro pension system

The micro pension scheme was implemented in 2014 to support the self-employed and entrepreneurs in Nigeria. In short, it provides greater flexibility to tradespeople, professionals, entrepreneurs and self-employed workers who may not qualify for a pension plan due to nonengagement in conventional jobs. But it is based on the basic principle of putting a certain limit in the pension account.

4. Individual Retirement Account (IRA):
   - Traditional IRA: Students with earned income can contribute to a Traditional IRA and potentially deduct contributions from their taxable income. Taxes on earnings are deferred until withdrawals during retirement.
   - Roth IRA: While contributions to a Roth IRA are not tax-deductible, qualified withdrawals during retirement are tax-free. This can be advantageous for students in lower tax brackets now, who expect to be in higher tax brackets during retirement.

5. Employer-Sponsored Retirement Plans:
   - If you work part-time or have a job with an employer that offers a retirement plan like a 401(k), take advantage of it. Contribute enough to receive any employer match, as it's essentially free money.

6. SEP-IRA (Simplified Employee Pension IRA):
   - If you have self-employment income, a SEP-IRA can be an option for retirement savings. It allows contributions based on a percentage of your earnings, up to a certain limit.

7. Solo 401(k):
   - If you're self-employed or running a small business, a Solo 401(k) is a retirement savings option that enables you to contribute as both the employer and the employee.

8. High-Yield Savings Account:
   - While not specifically designed for retirement savings, a high-yield savings account can be a good place to park money for short-term financial goals and act as an emergency fund.

9. Taxable Investment Accounts:
   - While not retirement-specific, taxable investment accounts can still be used to save and invest money. Although they don't offer the same tax advantages as retirement accounts, they provide flexibility for accessing funds before retirement age.

Remember that the amount you can contribute to retirement accounts may be limited by your earned income or the specific account type. Additionally, your financial situation and goals will influence which retirement savings options are most suitable for you. Before making any decisions, consider consulting a financial advisor to determine the best approach for your individual circumstances and to ensure your retirement savings align with your long-term financial goals.

C. Creating a financial roadmap for life after graduation

Creating a financial roadmap for life after graduation is essential for students to transition smoothly into the next phase of their lives. It involves planning and setting clear financial goals to achieve long-term financial success. These are some ways you can explore in creating a financial roadmap:

1. Assessing Financial Situation:
   - Evaluate current financial status, including savings, debts, and expenses, to understand the starting point for building a financial plan.

2. Setting Short and Long-Term Goals:
   - Define short-term goals like paying off any debt, student loans or finding a job after graduation, as well as long-term goals like saving for a down payment on a home or retirement.

3. Creating a Budget:
   - Develop a budget to manage post-graduation income and expenses. Prioritize essential expenses while leaving room for savings and discretionary spending.

4. Emergency Fund:
   - Establish an emergency fund to cover unexpected expenses and provide a safety net during the transition from college to the workforce.

5. Managing Student Loans:
   - Understand student loan repayment options and create a plan to manage and pay off student loans responsibly.

6. Exploring Employment Benefits:
   - Assess job offers and their benefits packages, including retirement plans, health insurance, and other perks that impact your financial well-being.

7. Contributing to Retirement Accounts:
   - If possible, start contributing to retirement accounts like micro pension scheme, a 401(k) or IRA as early as feasible to take advantage of compounding growth.

8. Paying Off High-Interest Debts:
   - Prioritize paying off high-interest debts, such as credit card balances, to avoid unnecessary interest expenses.

9. Seeking Financial Advice:
   - Consult a financial advisor to seek guidance on creating a personalized financial plan that aligns with your goals and circumstances.

10. Building Credit:
    - Start building a positive credit history by responsibly using credit and paying bills on time, which can be beneficial for future financial opportunities.

11. Planning for Housing:

- Determine housing options after graduation, whether it's renting, buying, or moving back home temporarily.

12. Investing in Professional Development:
- Invest in further education, certifications, or skills development to enhance career prospects and earning potential.

Remember that creating a financial roadmap is an ongoing process that may require adjustments as life circumstances change. Regularly review and update your financial plan, stay disciplined in managing finances, and seek support and advice when needed to ensure a financially secure and successful future after graduation.

Chapter VII
NAVIGATING FINANCIAL CHALLENGES

As a student, navigating financial challenges involve taking proactive steps to manage your finances effectively and overcome difficulties. These are some strategies to help you cope with financial challenges:

1. Assess the Situation: Take a comprehensive look at your financial situation, including income, expenses, debts, and savings. Understanding where you stand financially is the first step to finding solutions.

2. Create a Budget: Develop a detailed budget to track income and expenses. Identify areas where spending can be reduced and allocate money wisely towards essential needs and savings.

3. Prioritize Essential Expenses: Ensure that necessities like housing, food, utilities, and education-related costs are covered before discretionary spending.

4. Seek Additional Income: Build and create a side hustle, explore part-time work, freelance opportunities, or gig jobs to supplement your income and ease financial strain.

5. Use Student Resources: Take advantage of student resources such as scholarships, grants, work-study programs, and financial aid offices to help ease the burden of educational expenses.

6. Communicate with Creditors: If you are facing difficulties in making debt payments, communicate with creditors to discuss possible payment plans or deferment options.

7. Avoid High-Interest Debt: Be cautious with credit cards and avoid accumulating high-interest debt that can exacerbate financial challenges.

8. Build an Emergency Fund: Start saving a small portion of your income regularly to build an emergency fund that can cover unexpected expenses.

9. Utilize Community Resources: Check if there are community resources or non-profit organizations that provide assistance with basic needs like food, housing, or utility bills.

10. Seek Financial Counseling: Consider seeking guidance from a financial counselor or advisor who can provide personalized advice and strategies to improve your financial situation.

11. Avoid Impulse Spending: Stay disciplined with your spending habits and avoid impulsive purchases that can strain your budget.

12. Focus on Long-Term Goals: Keep your long-term financial goals in mind and remain committed to your education and career aspirations.

Remember that financial challenges are temporary, and taking proactive steps to manage them can lead to improved financial well-being. It's essential to stay positive, seek support from friends, family, or counselors, and make informed decisions about your finances. By implementing these strategies, you can navigate financial challenges and work towards a more stable and secure financial future.

A. Dealing with unexpected financial setbacks

Dealing with unexpected financial setbacks can be challenging for you as a student. However, with careful planning and a proactive approach, you can effectively navigate these situations. These are some steps to cope with unexpected financial setbacks:

1. Stay Calm and Assess the Situation: Take a deep breath and remain calm. Evaluate the extent of the setback and its impact on your finances.

2. Revisit Your Budget: Review your budget and identify areas where you can cut back on non-essential expenses to free up funds for addressing the setback.

3. Prioritize Essential Expenses: Ensure that critical expenses like housing, utilities, and food are covered first.

4. Seek Support: Reach out to family, friends, or a financial advisor for guidance and support. Sometimes, discussing your situation with others can provide valuable insights and potential solutions.

5. Utilize Emergency Fund: If you have an emergency fund, consider using it to address immediate financial needs. If you

don't have one, start building one for future unexpected situations.

6. Communicate with Creditors: If you are unable to make debt payments on time, communicate with creditors to discuss temporary payment arrangements or hardship options.

7. Explore Financial Aid: Check if you are eligible for additional financial aid, grants, or scholarships to help cover unexpected expenses.

8. Consider Part-Time Work: Look for part-time work or engagement opportunities to supplement your income during this challenging period.

9. Evaluate Student Loan Repayment Options: If you have student loans, explore repayment options such as income-driven repayment plans or deferment if you are experiencing financial hardship.

10. Delay Non-Essential Expenses: Postpone non-essential expenses or discretionary spending until your financial situation stabilizes.

11. Stay Focused on Academic Goals: Despite the setback, remain focused on your academic goals and continue working towards your degree or career aspirations.

12. Be Patient and Persistent: Financial setbacks can be temporary. Stay persistent in finding solutions and remain patient as you work towards financial recovery.

Remember that dealing with unexpected financial setbacks is a common part of life, and it's essential not to be too hard on yourself during these times. Be proactive in finding solutions, seek support when needed, and stay positive about your ability to overcome the challenges. By taking thoughtful actions and staying resilient, you can successfully manage unexpected financial setbacks and move forward towards a more stable financial future.

B. Strategies for managing financial stress as a student

Managing financial stress as a student requires a combination of practical strategies and mental well-being techniques. These are some strategies to help you cope with financial stress:

1. Create a Budget: Develop a budget to track income and expenses, prioritize essential expenses, and allocate funds wisely. A well-organized budget can reduce uncertainty and anxiety about finances.

2. Seek Financial Aid and Scholarships: Explore available financial aid options, grants, and scholarships to ease the financial burden of education expenses.

3. Part-Time Work: Consider part-time work or engagement opportunities to supplement your income and cover essential expenses.

4. Build an Emergency Fund: Start saving regularly to build an emergency fund that can provide a safety net for unexpected expenses and reduce financial stress.

5. Limit Credit Card Use: Avoid accumulating credit card debt, as high-interest rates can exacerbate financial stress. Use credit cards responsibly and pay off the balance each month if possible.

6. Communicate with Creditors: If you are struggling to make debt payments, reach out to creditors to discuss payment options or temporary hardship arrangements.

7. Use Campus Resources: Many universities offer financial counseling services or student support centers that can provide guidance and resources for managing financial stress.

8. Practice Stress-Relief Techniques: Engage in stress-relief activities like meditation, exercise, or spending time in nature to manage stress and promote mental well-being.

9. Focus on Priorities: Identify and prioritize essential needs over wants, and avoid unnecessary spending during financially challenging periods.

10. Limit Comparisons: Avoid comparing your financial situation to that of others, as it can lead to unnecessary stress and feelings of inadequacy.

11. Seek Emotional Support: Talk to friends, family, or a counselor about your financial stress. Sharing your feelings can be therapeutic and help you gain new perspectives.

12. Break Tasks into Smaller Steps: If financial stress feels overwhelming, break tasks into smaller, manageable steps to address one thing at a time.

13. Stay Positive and Persistent: Cultivate a positive mindset and stay persistent in finding solutions. Remember that financial stress is temporary, and taking proactive steps can lead to improvements.

14. Focus on Academics: Stay focused on your academic goals and invest in your education, as it can lead to better financial opportunities in the future.

15. Celebrate Small Wins: Acknowledge and celebrate even small financial achievements, as this can boost motivation and reduce stress.

By implementing these strategies and adopting a proactive approach to managing financial stress, you can build resilience and work towards a healthier financial mindset. Remember that it's okay to seek help and support during challenging times, and taking care of your mental well-being is as important as managing your finances.

C. Seeking professional financial advice when needed

Seeking professional financial advice as a student can provide numerous benefits and be a valuable investment in your financial future. These are some compelling reasons why you may need to seek professional financial advice:

1. Personalized Guidance: A financial advisor can provide personalized advice tailored to your unique financial situation, goals, and risk tolerance. They can help create a financial plan that aligns with your aspirations.

2. Comprehensive Financial Planning: A professional financial advisor can offer a holistic approach to financial planning, covering various aspects such as budgeting, saving, investing, managing debt, and retirement planning.

3. Long-Term Perspective: Financial advisors can help you develop a long-term perspective by emphasizing the importance of early savings and investments, which can lead to significant growth over time.

4. Student Loan Management: A financial advisor can assist in understanding student loan options, repayment plans, and strategies to manage student debt effectively.

5. Investment Strategies: Understanding different investment options and their risk-return profiles can be challenging. An advisor can help you make informed investment decisions that suit your financial goals and risk tolerance.

6. Tax Efficiency: Financial advisors can provide insights into tax-efficient investment strategies and help you take advantage of available tax benefits and deductions.

7. Retirement Planning: Although retirement may seem distant for students, starting early can significantly impact future financial security. An advisor can help set retirement goals and develop a plan to achieve them.

8. Insurance and Risk Management: An advisor can assess the need for insurance coverage, such as health, life, or disability insurance, to protect against unexpected financial setbacks.

9. Decision Making Support: When facing significant financial decisions, having an expert to guide you can reduce stress and provide confidence in making well-informed choices.

10. Education and Empowerment: Financial advisors can educate you about essential financial concepts, helping you to develop a better understanding of money management and financial independence.

11. Handling Windfalls: If you receive a windfall, such as an inheritance or a large scholarship, a financial advisor can assist in managing it wisely and making strategic decisions.

12. Building Financial Confidence: By having a professional advisor to consult, you can gain confidence in managing your finances and build a strong foundation for financial success.

It's essential to find a reputable and qualified financial advisor who works in your best interest and charges transparent fees. While seeking more knowledge and professional financial advice may involve some costs, the potential benefits and peace of mind it provides can be well worth the investment in the long run.

Chapter VIII
REAL-LIFE CASE STUDIES

Let me give you these real-life examples of students who have built a strong foundation of financial freedom. Keep in mind that these examples are to guide you in your pursuit of a foundation for financial freedom:

Case Study 1: John – He is an Early Savvy Investor.
John, a university student, started investing in the stock market during his freshman year. He researched investment strategies, diversified his portfolio, and consistently contributed a portion of his part-time job income to his investments. Over the years, John benefited from the power of compounding and witnessed his investment grow significantly. By the time he graduated, John had accumulated a sizable investment portfolio, setting him on the path to financial freedom.

Case Study 2: Bolade adopted Budgeting and Debt Management strategy.
Bolade, a graduate student, managed his finances diligently during his academic years. He created a detailed budget, prioritized essential expenses, and lived within his means. Bolade also took advantage of financial aid and scholarships to minimize his exposure to debts and student loan debt. After graduating, he continued to live frugally, directing his surplus income towards investing into the future and building his investment aggressively. Within a few years, Bolade became debt-free, and the disciplined financial habits he developed allowed him to save and invest for his future with ease.

Case Study 3: Sarah built an Entrepreneurship Mindset.
Sarah, an undergraduate student with a passion for entrepreneurship, launched a successful online business during her university years. Through hard work and dedication, her business thrived, providing a steady stream of income. Sarah wisely reinvested a portion of her profits to expand her business while also saving and investing for personal financial goals. By the time she graduated, Sarah's business had become a stable source of income, allowing her the financial freedom to pursue her dreams.

Case Study 4: Alex – He is a Goal-Oriented Planner.
Alex, a medical school student, was committed to achieving financial freedom despite the high cost of education. He set clear financial goals, including minimizing any debt exposure, building an emergency fund, and contributing to micro retirement accounts early on. Through careful planning, budgeting, and working part-time, Alex managed to cover a significant portion of his education expenses without excessive debt. His strategic approach to financial management allowed him to graduate with a strong financial foundation and peace of mind.

Case Study 5: Sola developed Goal-Oriented mindset with clear vision.
I started my academic journey as a student with Goal-Oriented mindset and clear vision. I desired to pursue my career in the private sector of the economy where there were opportunities for high paying jobs. This goal prompted me to decide that I must come out of school with good grades and also acquire

professional qualifications. By the grace of God, I graduated with good grades, acquired professional Master degree and became a chartered accountant of high repute.

Remember that achieving financial freedom is a unique journey for each individual, and success depends on personal circumstances, goals, and decisions. These case studies highlight the importance of disciplined financial habits, long-term planning, and wise decision-making in building a strong foundation of financial freedom for you.

A. Common Points in the Success stories of students who achieved financial freedom

The case studies above are some inspiring success stories of students and young individuals who have attained financial freedom through hard work, discipline, and strategic financial planning. These stories often highlight the importance of early financial literacy, wise money management, and a long-term perspective. These are some common points found in success stories of students who achieved financial freedom:

1. Early Savvy Investors: Some students start investing early in life, leveraging the power of compound interest to grow their money over time. By making informed investment decisions and remaining patient, these individuals build substantial wealth that contributes to their financial freedom.

2. Entrepreneurial Success: Students who start successful businesses during their academic years or shortly after graduation often achieve financial freedom at a young age. By identifying market opportunities and providing innovative solutions, these entrepreneurs generate significant income and build successful ventures.

3. Budgeting and Debt Management Experts: Students who master budgeting and diligently manage their debts early on can pay off loans faster and avoid excessive interest expenses. This financial discipline sets them on a path to financial freedom sooner.

4. Education and Career Advancement: Some students prioritize their education and career advancement, leading to higher earning potential in their chosen professions. By making strategic career choices, they can secure well-paying jobs and improve their financial prospects.

5. Multiple Income Streams: Students who explore various income-generating opportunities, such as freelancing, part-time work, or investments, can accumulate multiple income streams that contribute to financial freedom.

6. Frugal Living and Delayed Gratification: Individuals who adopt frugal living habits and practice delayed gratification resist unnecessary expenses and prioritize saving and investing for the future. Over time, their disciplined approach leads to financial independence.

7. Real Estate Investments: Some students invest in real estate properties, either by purchasing rental properties or through real estate crowdfunding platforms. These investments can provide a steady stream of passive income, contributing to their financial freedom.

It's important to remember that financial freedom is a journey that requires dedication, perseverance, and prudent decision-making. Every individual's path to financial freedom is unique, and what works for one person may not work for another. Aspiring to achieve financial freedom is commendable, and it's essential to set realistic goals, stay committed to financial discipline, and continually educate yourself about personal finance and investing.

B. Learning from the experiences of others

You can learn valuable lessons and gain insights by learning from the experiences of others. These are some ways to do so:

1. Reading Success Stories: Read books, articles, or interviews featuring successful individuals who have achieved their goals, overcome challenges, or made significant accomplishments. These stories can inspire and offer practical advice.

2. Seeking Mentors: Connect with mentors or experienced professionals in fields of interest. Learning from their experiences can provide guidance, support, and valuable insights for your own journey.

3. Networking: Engage in networking events, workshops, or conferences where you can meet and learn from people with diverse backgrounds and experiences.

4. Joining Student Organizations: Participate in student organizations related to your interests or career goals. Engaging with like-minded peers can expose you to different perspectives and experiences.

5. Listening to Guest Speakers: Attend seminars or lectures featuring guest speakers who share their experiences and expertise. These events often provide valuable life and career lessons.

6. Online Forums and Communities: Join online forums or social media groups focused on topics of interest. Engaging in discussions with others can expand your knowledge and understanding.

7. Internships and Job Shadows: Seek opportunities for internships or job shadows to gain practical experience and learn from professionals in your desired field.

8. Reflecting on Personal Mistakes: Reflect on your own experiences and mistakes. Learning from your own challenges and successes can lead to personal growth and improvement.

9. Observing Role Models: Observe and learn from role models, both within and outside your immediate circle. It can be anyone

you admire, whether a family member, teacher, celebrity, or historical figure.

10. Keeping an Open Mind: Be open to different perspectives and experiences. Embrace diversity and consider alternative approaches to learning and problem-solving.

11. Emphasizing Empathy: Practice empathy and actively listen to others' stories. Understanding their perspectives can broaden your understanding of different situations.

12. Asking for Advice: Don't hesitate to ask for advice and guidance from those you trust. Seeking input from others can provide valuable insights and help you make informed decisions.

Learning from the experiences of others is a powerful way to expand your knowledge, gain new perspectives, and avoid repeating mistakes. It allows you to benefit from the wisdom and insights of those who have already walked similar paths, empowering you to make better-informed decisions and navigate your own journey more effectively.

Chapter IX
TOOLS AND RESOURCES

Understanding the tools and resources applicable for you as a student is essential for enhancing your learning, productivity, and overall well-being. These tools are to serve as a guide and can assist with academic tasks, financial management, organization, and personal development. These are some key categories of tools and resources applicable to you:

1. Academic Tools:
   - Online Research Databases: Access to digital libraries, research papers, and scholarly articles to support academic studies.
   - Citation Generators: Tools that help create proper citations and references for academic papers.
   - Grammar and Plagiarism Checkers: Tools to proofread and ensure academic integrity in writing.
   - Note-Taking Apps: Digital platforms for organizing and managing class notes efficiently.
   - Online Learning Platforms: Platforms offering courses and educational content in various subjects.

2. Productivity Tools:
   - Calendar and Scheduling Apps: Tools to manage daily schedules, deadlines, and appointments.
   - To-Do List Apps: Platforms to create and track tasks, assignments, and projects.
   - Time Management Techniques: Techniques like the Pomodoro Technique to enhance productivity and focus.

- Collaboration Tools: Software that facilitates group projects and teamwork.

3. Financial Management Resources:
  - Budgeting Apps: Tools for creating and managing budgets to track expenses and savings.
  - Personal Finance Websites: Websites offering financial advice, tips, and resources for students.
  - Scholarship Search Engines: Platforms to find scholarship opportunities and financial aid information.

4. Mental Health and Well-being Resources:
  - Meditation Apps: Apps providing guided meditation and relaxation techniques to manage stress.
  - Mental Health Support: Resources like counseling services or helplines for emotional support.

5. Career Development Resources:
  - Job Search Platforms: Websites for finding internships, part-time jobs, or full-time employment.
  - Career Counseling Services: Support for exploring career options and guidance for career development.

6. Language Learning Tools:
  - Language Learning Apps: Apps to practice and improve language skills in multiple languages.

7. Online Learning Resources:
  - Massive Open Online Courses (MOOCs): Platforms offering free or affordable online courses in various subjects.

8. Networking Platforms:
   - LinkedIn: Professional networking platform for connecting with peers and potential employers.

9. Health and Fitness Apps:
   - Fitness Trackers: Apps for monitoring physical activity and maintaining a healthy lifestyle.
   - Nutrition Apps: Tools for tracking and managing dietary choices.

Understanding and effectively utilizing these tools and resources can significantly enhance your learning experience, personal growth, and overall success. Being proactive in seeking out and utilizing these resources can help you to make the most of your academic journey and prepare you for future challenges and opportunities.

A. Recommended financial apps and tools for students

There are several excellent financial apps and tools available that can help you to manage your finances, budget effectively, and plan for your financial future. These are some recommended financial apps and tools for you:

1. Mint: Mint is a popular budgeting app that allows you to track expenses, set budgets, and receive alerts when you approach your spending limits.

2. PocketGuard: PocketGuard is another budgeting app that helps you stay on top of your finances by tracking your income, expenses, and savings goals.

3. Acorns: Acorns is an investment app that rounds up your purchases to the nearest dollar and invests the spare change in a diversified portfolio.

4. Robinhood: Robinhood is a commission-free investing app that allows you to buy and sell stocks, ETFs, and cryptocurrencies.

5. Venmo: Venmo is a peer-to-peer payment app that allows you to easily send and receive money from friends and family.

6. Splitwise: Splitwise is a handy app for tracking shared expenses among roommates or friends, making it easier to split bills and settle debts.

7. Goodbudget: Goodbudget is a budgeting app based on the envelope budgeting system, which helps you allocate funds to different spending categories.

8. TurboTax: TurboTax is a tax preparation app that guides you through the process of filing your tax returns accurately.

9. Wally: Wally is a personal finance app that helps you track expenses, set financial goals, and monitor your progress.

10. Fudget: Fudget is a simple and user-friendly app for creating and managing budgets without unnecessary complexities.

11. You Need a Budget (YNAB): YNAB is a comprehensive budgeting app that encourages users to assign every dollar a job and prioritize savings and debt repayment.

12. Student Loan Hero: Student Loan Hero is a helpful app that assists students in managing their student loans by offering personalized repayment strategies and resources.

Before choosing an app, consider its security features, user reviews, and whether it aligns with your financial needs and goals. Remember that while these apps can be valuable tools, personal finance ultimately requires discipline and responsible money management. Using these apps in conjunction with sound financial habits can significantly improve your financial well-being as a student.

B. Useful websites and books for further learning

There are numerous useful websites and books that can provide further learning on financial freedom for students. These are some recommended resources:

Websites:
1. Investopedia (www.investopedia.com): A comprehensive financial education website with articles, tutorials, and guides on various personal finance topics, including investing, budgeting, and retirement planning.

2. The Balance (www.thebalance.com): Offers practical advice and resources on money management, saving, and investing for students and young adults.

3. NerdWallet (www.nerdwallet.com): Provides unbiased financial guidance, tools, and calculators to help students make informed financial decisions.

4. Khan Academy (www.khanacademy.org): Offers free online courses on personal finance, investing, and economics.

5. Smart About Money (www.smartaboutmoney.org): A website offering free courses and resources on budgeting, credit management, and financial planning.

Books:
1. "The Total Money Makeover" by Dave Ramsey: Provides a step-by-step plan for getting out of debt, building an emergency fund, and achieving financial independence.

2. "Rich Dad Poor Dad" by Robert T. Kiyosaki: Offers valuable lessons on money management, investing, and building wealth.

3. "The Automatic Millionaire" by David Bach: Explores the concept of paying yourself first and creating automatic savings plans to achieve financial freedom.

4. "I Will Teach You to Be Rich" by Ramit Sethi: A practical guide to personal finance, budgeting, investing, and earning more money.

5. "The Millionaire Next Door" by Thomas J. Stanley and William D. Danko: Examines the habits and characteristics of self-made millionaires and how they achieved financial success.

6. "Broke Millennial: Stop Scraping By and Get Your Financial Life Together" by Erin Lowry: Geared specifically towards young adults, this book offers practical advice for managing money and building financial security.

7. "Your Money or Your Life" by Vicki Robin and Joe Dominguez: Explores the concept of financial independence and how to achieve it through conscious spending and saving.

These resources can serve as valuable tools for you, as you are looking to gain a deeper understanding of personal finance, investing, and building a strong foundation for financial freedom. Remember to complement your learning with hands-on practice and practical application to make the most of these valuable insights.

Chapter X
PRACTICAL STRATEGIES TO ACHIEVE FINANCIAL FREEDOM

When you are planning for your financial freedom as a student, you need to take a closer look at the opportunities that are available for you to quicken your journey to financial freedom in life. These are the practical strategies that can aid your plan to achieve financial freedom:

A- Increase your Income at your Current Job.
When you graduate from the university and you do not get a high paying job, there will be a need for you to plan for a way to increase your income in your current job. You may consider the following strategies:

1. Showcase Your Value: Demonstrate your skills, accomplishments, and the positive impact you've had on the company. Highlight how you've gone above and beyond your responsibilities to contribute to the organization's success.

2. Set Goals and Objectives: Work with your supervisor to establish clear, measurable goals that align with the company's objectives. Meeting or exceeding these goals can strengthen your case for a pay increase.

3. Seek Feedback and Improve: Regularly seek feedback from your superiors and colleagues to identify areas for improvement. Addressing constructive criticism shows your commitment to growth and development.

4. Take on More Responsibilities: Volunteer for additional projects or responsibilities that align with your skills and interests. Showing initiative can lead to recognition and potential salary adjustments.

5. Quantify Your Achievements: Whenever possible, quantify the results of your work. Use data and metrics to demonstrate the value you've brought to the company.

6. Stay Updated: Keep yourself informed about industry trends and advancements in your field. Continuous learning can make you more valuable to the company.

7. Negotiate During Performance Reviews: When you have performance reviews or evaluations, use this opportunity to discuss your compensation. Present your achievements and contributions to justify a salary increase.

8. Research Salary Data: Gather information about the average salary for your role and experience level in your industry and location. This data can support your case during salary discussions.

9. Seek Internal Opportunities: Explore internal job openings within your company. Moving to a higher-paying role can be easier if you've already proven yourself as a valuable employee.

10. Promote Your Soft Skills: Highlight your leadership, teamwork, and problem-solving skills. These soft skills are highly valued by employers and can contribute to salary adjustments.

Remember that salary negotiations require tact and diplomacy. Be confident but respectful when discussing your pay. It's essential to know your worth and be able to articulate the value you bring to the organization. If you've followed all the strategies above and your salary hasn't increased, you may need to look for a job at another company or a higher position at another company with higher salaries. This leads us to the next strategy.

B- Get a High Paying Job.
Securing a high-paying job often requires a combination of strategic planning, education, experience, and networking. These are some strategies to increase your chances of landing a high-paying job:

1. Education and Skill Development: Obtain relevant education and certifications that align with high-demand industries or specialized fields. Continuous skill development and staying updated on industry trends are essential.

2. Choose In-Demand Industries: Focus on industries that have a higher demand for skilled professionals and offer competitive salaries.

3. Gain Experience: Seek internships, part-time jobs, or volunteer opportunities to gain practical experience in your chosen field.

Relevant experience can make you more attractive to potential employers.

4. Network: Build a professional network by attending industry events, job fairs, and networking with peers, mentors, and professionals in your field. Networking can open doors to hidden job opportunities.

5. Personal Branding: Create a strong online presence through LinkedIn and other professional platforms. Showcase your skills, accomplishments, and expertise to attract potential employers.

6. Research Companies: Identify companies known for offering high salaries and excellent benefits. Tailor your job search to target these organizations.

7. Negotiate: When you receive a job offer, don't hesitate to negotiate your salary and benefits. Research market rates and be prepared to showcase your value to the company.

8. Demonstrate Value: During interviews, emphasize your skills and accomplishments that align with the company's needs. Show how you can contribute to their success.

9. Be Flexible: Consider relocation if high-paying opportunities are more prevalent in certain regions. Being open to new locations can increase your options.

10. Develop Soft Skills: Along with technical skills, cultivate strong communication, leadership, problem-solving, and teamwork abilities. Employers value these qualities in candidates.

Remember, landing a high-paying job may take some time and effort. Be consistent, persistent, stay proactive in your job search, and continue honing your skills to make yourself a competitive candidate in the job market.

C- Side Hustle Ideas
These are some suitable side hustles for students that can vary depending on your skills, interests, and available time. These side hustle ideas can also be helpful when you are not having a high paying job. These are some ideas:

1. Freelance Writing or Editing: If you have strong writing or editing skills, you can offer your services to individuals or businesses for content creation or proofreading.

2. Tutoring: Share your knowledge in subjects you excel in by offering tutoring services to fellow students or younger students.

3. Graphic Design: If you're skilled in graphic design, you can create logos, social media graphics, or design websites for clients.

4. Photography: If you have a talent for photography, consider offering portrait sessions or event photography.

5. Online Surveys or Microtasks: Participate in online surveys or complete microtasks on platforms that offer compensation.

6. Social Media Management: Help businesses or influencers manage their social media accounts and create engaging content.

7. Pet Sitting or Dog Walking: If you're an animal lover, offer pet sitting or dog walking services in your neighborhood.

8. Selling Handmade Crafts: If you're crafty, you can sell handmade items on platforms like Etsy.

9. Language Translation: If you're bilingual or multilingual, offer translation services for documents or online content.

10. Virtual Assistance: Assist busy professionals or entrepreneurs with tasks such as data entry, scheduling, or email management.

Remember to consider your skills, interests, and schedule when choosing a side hustle. It should be something you enjoy and can manage alongside your studies.

D- Investment and Launch of Business.

This investment options are to guide you with the required information to understand the various investment opportunities that you can leverage on as a student and after graduation to achieve financial freedom. The best investing strategies increase returns, minimize risk and meet your financial goals. You need to find the strategy that's right and will work for your financial goals. An investment strategy is a way of thinking that shapes how you select the investments in your portfolio. The best strategies should help you meet your financial goals and grow your wealth while maintaining a level of risk that lets you sleep at night. The strategy you choose may influence everything from what types of assets you have to, how you approach buying and selling those assets.

If you're ready to start investing, a good rule of thumb is to ask yourself some basic questions: What are my goals? How much time do I plan to attain financial freedom? How comfortable am I with risk taken? Do I know how much I want to invest in stocks, bonds or an alternative?

Below are some investment options:
1- Investment Savings Account
Investment savings account pays a high interest rate and gives you easy access to your money with no maturity dates.

Saving can also mean putting your money into products such as a bank time account. Investing using some of your money with the aim of helping to make it grow by buying assets that might increase in value, such as stocks, property or shares in a mutual fund.

An investment account holds cash and the investments (stocks, bonds, ETFs, mutual funds, etc.) that you buy and sell to realize your financial goals.

Savings accounts offer one of the simplest ways to earn interest on the money you have. They offer higher interest rates than a regular checking account, while still making it easy to spend and withdraw money. However, savings account rates are much lower than other investments, and they don't keep pace with inflation.

Types of savings accounts:
- Regular savings account: earns interest and offers quick access to funds.

☐ Money market account: earns interest and may provide cheque writing privileges and ATM access.

☐ Certificate of deposit, or CD: usually has the highest interest rate among savings accounts, but no access to funds.

2- Shares

Share is part or portion of a larger amount which is divided among a number of people, or to which a number of people contribute.

"Under the proposals, investors would pay a greater share of the annual fees required"

Shares represent ownership of a company. When an individual buys shares in a company, he becomes one of its owners. Shareholders choose who runs a company and are involved in making key decisions, such as whether a business should be sold or venture in an expansion plan.

A company may issue different types (also known as "classes") of shares. These can include:

a. Ordinary Shares

Ordinary shares are the most common type of shares. They typically carry voting rights but do not give shareholders rights to receive or demand for dividends.

Ordinary shareholders also receive less dividends compared to shareholders who hold preference shares. Companies may divide their ordinary shares into different classes (e.g., "A" and "B") with different rights attached to each class.

b. Preference Shares

Preference shares confer some preferential rights on the holder, superior to ordinary shares. Normally, the preferential rights are the rights to fixed dividends, priority to dividends over ordinary shares and to a return of capital when the company goes into liquidation.

c. Redeemable Preference Shares.
Redeemable preference shares allow for the repayment of the principal share capital to shareholders. The company may redeem these shares at an agreed value on a specified date or at the discretion of the directors. This is on the condition that the company is a going concern.
Any redemptions can be paid out of the company's capital using proceeds from a fresh issue of shares.

d. Convertible Preference Shares
Convertible preference shares usually carry rights to a fixed dividend for a particular term. At the end of the term, the company can choose to convert it into ordinary shares or leave them as they are. Conversion prices must be specified in the company's constitution. If the price of an ordinary share rises, the conversion prices will not follow. It is essentially allowing the shareholder to purchase ordinary shares at a lower price. The relevant transaction is in "Conversion of Shares".

e. Treasury Shares
Treasury shares are ordinary shares which the company acquired from shareholders. While the company is listed as the owner of the treasury shares, it is not allowed to exercise the right to attend or vote at meetings, and no dividends may be paid to the company.
The total number of treasury shares held by the company is capped at 10% of the total number of ordinary shares issued. Any excess treasury shares (i.e., more than 10% of the total number of

ordinary shares) must be cancelled or disposed of within 6 months.

3- Bonds

A bond is a debt security, similar to an IOU. Borrowers issue bonds to raise money from investors willing to lend them money for a certain amount of time. When you buy a bond, you are lending to the issuer, which may be a government, municipality, or corporation.

A bond is a fixed-income instrument that represents a loan made by an investor to a borrower (typically corporate or governmental). A bond could be thought of as an I.O.U. between the lender and borrower that includes the details of the loan and its payments.

2 ways to make money on bonds are:

- Interest payments. With most bonds, you'll get regular interest payments while you hold the bond. Most bonds have a fixed interest rate.
- Selling a bond for more than you paid. In general, when interest rates go down, bond prices go up.

By buying a bond, you're giving the issuer a loan, and they agree to pay you back the face value of the loan on a specific date, and to pay you periodic interest payments along the way, usually twice a year. Unlike stocks, bonds issued by companies give you no ownership rights.

4- Mutual funds

A mutual fund is an investment fund that pools money from many investors to purchase securities. The term is typically used in the United States, Canada, India, and Nigeria while similar structures across the globe include the SICAV in Europe and open-ended investment company in the UK.

A mutual fund is a pool of money managed by a professional Fund Manager. It is a trust that collects money from a number of investors who share a common investment objective and invests the same in equities, bonds, money market instruments and/or other securities.

Mutual funds let you pool your money with other investors to "mutually" buy stocks, bonds, and other investments. They're run by professional money managers who decide which securities to buy (stocks, bonds, etc.) and when to sell them. You get exposure to all the investments in the fund and any income they generate.

Most mutual funds fall into one of four main categories: money market funds, bond funds, stock funds, and target date funds. Each type has different features, risks, and rewards.

One can invest in mutual funds by submitting a duly completed application form along with a cheque or bank draft at the branch office or designated Investor Service Centers (ISC) of mutual Funds or Registrar & Transfer Agents of the respective mutual funds.

5-   Commercial papers

Commercial paper is an unsecured, short-term debt instrument issued by corporations. It's typically used to finance short-term liabilities such as payroll, accounts payable, and inventories. Commercial paper is usually issued at a discount from face value. It reflects prevailing market interest rates.

The two basic types of commercial paper are drafts and notes. The note is a two-party instrument whereby one person (maker) promises to pay money to a second person (payee). The draft is a three-party instrument whereby one person (drawer) directs a second (drawee) to pay money to the third (payee).

6-   Treasury Bill

Treasury Bills are short term instruments issued by CBN on behalf of FGN at a discount. These do not yield any interest but are issued at a discount and repaid at par when it gets matured.
Description and Features:
Tenors for T-bills in the primary market are 91 days, 182 days and 364 days. The secondary market ranges from 7 days to 363 days
Individuals, firms, companies, and financial institutions are eligible to invest in treasury bills.
T-bills are issued at a discount but redeemed at par. Priced in units of N1,000.
The repayment of the bill is made at par on the maturity of the term.
Treasury bills are highly liquid negotiable instruments, that are available in both primary and secondary markets.

Benefits
Relatively low-risk option.
Interest received not subject to tax.
Repayment guaranteed at maturity.
Used as collateral securities.
Interest with the principal can be re-invested immediately.

7-   Business
To launch your own business successfully.
These are eleven basic steps that will guarantee your success:

1. Develop the leader within through self-mastery tools to Invent or Reinvent yourself.
2. Know and accept yourself as an entrepreneur before you start.
3. Generate Business ideas.
4. Research the validity of your business ideas.
5. Test your business premise in the real world.
6. Develop SMART Business plan.
7. Set up the right Business framework.
8. Understand your financials, accounting and tax obligations.
9. Develop your Business Model.
10. Breakdown your Business Model into Milestones for Execution.
11. Then Launch your Business.

8- Economic Assets such as Real Estates, Gold etc.
Economic assets are entities functioning as stores of value and over which ownership rights are enforced by institutional units, individually or collectively, and from which economic benefits may be derived by their owners by holding them, or using them, over a period of time.

An asset is an entity from which the economic owner can derive a benefit or series of benefits in future accounting periods by holding or using the entity over a period of time, or from which the economic owner has derived a benefit in past periods and is still receiving a benefit in the current period.

An asset is anything that has current or future economic value. Examples include Real Estate, Gold, and Investments.

Gold as a financial asset.

Unlike other commodities, gold does not get used up or consumed, imbuing the precious metal with a sense of everlasting value. Gold serves as a hedge against the declining value of currencies through inflation, which leads many investors to consider gold an alternative asset and a way of safeguarding their wealth.

Gold is often considered a good investment for diversification, as it may be less correlated with other assets such as stocks or bonds. This means that the price of gold may be less affected by movements in other asset classes, which can help to reduce overall portfolio risk.

Gold and silver are tangible assets, but are frequently traded in the form of futures or options, which are financial derivatives.

Real Estate as an asset.

Real estate investing involves the purchase, management and sale or rental of real estate for profit. Someone who actively or passively invests in real estate is called a real estate entrepreneur or a real estate investor. Some investors actively develop, improve or renovate properties to make more money from them.

Real estate investing uses real estate properties as an investment vehicle and gains profit through a variety of methods. It can be as simple as owning real estate, collecting cash flow in rental income, and selling the asset for a higher price due to appreciation.

Apartment rentals, commercial real estate, land and crowdfunding platforms are all types of real estate investments.

Chapter XI
CONCLUSION

A quick recap on the Key Concepts on Finance for Students: Foundation for Financial Freedom are as follows:

1. Financial Education Importance: Understanding personal finance is crucial for you to make informed financial decisions and build a strong foundation for future financial freedom.

2. Budgeting and Expense Management: Creating a budget will help you to track income and expenses, prioritize essential needs, and allocate funds wisely.

3. Saving and Investing: Setting aside money for saving and investing early on will allow you to benefit from the power of compounding and build wealth over time.

4. Financial Goals: Setting clear financial goals will help you to stay focused and motivated on your journey towards financial freedom.

5. Managing Debt: Responsible debt management involves understanding student loans and credit card debt, paying off high-interest debt, and avoiding unnecessary borrowing.

6. Building Credit: Establishing and managing credit responsibly is essential for accessing future financial opportunities.

7. Emergency Fund: Having an emergency fund provides a safety net for unexpected expenses and financial setbacks.

8. Investing Basics: Understanding investment options, risk tolerance, and long-term vs. short-term strategies will empower you to make informed investment decisions.

9. Smart Money Habits: Cultivating frugal living, avoiding impulse spending, and embracing delayed gratification contribute to wise money management.

10. Retirement Planning: Planning for retirement early on will allow you to take advantage of time and compound interest to build a secure future.

11. Learning from Others: Gaining insights from success stories and experiences of others can provide valuable lessons and inspiration.

12. Seeking Professional Financial Advice: Consulting a financial advisor can offer personalized guidance and strategies to achieve financial goals.

My final thoughts for you on building a strong foundation for financial freedom.

Building a strong foundation for financial freedom as a student is a transformative journey that sets the stage for a secure and prosperous future. As you embark on this path, remember these final thoughts to guide you:

1. Start Early: Time is your most valuable asset when it comes to finances. Begin your financial journey as early as possible, and let the power of compounding work in your favor.

2. Educate Yourself: Take the time to learn about personal finance, budgeting, investing, and other essential financial concepts. Knowledge is the key to making informed decisions.

3. Set Clear Goals: Define your financial goals and create a roadmap to achieve them. Having a clear vision will keep you motivated and focused on your journey to financial freedom.

4. Live Within Your Means: Practice frugal living and avoid unnecessary expenses. Spend wisely and prioritize essential needs over wants.

5. Be Disciplined: Stay committed to your financial plan, even when it gets challenging. Discipline is the foundation of financial success.

6. Embrace Long-Term Thinking: Building financial freedom is not a quick fix; it's a lifelong commitment. Embrace a long-term perspective and be patient with your progress.

7. Manage Debt Responsibly: If you have loans or credit card debt, manage them responsibly and prioritize repayment.

8. Build an Emergency Fund: Creating an emergency fund provides financial security and prepares you for unexpected setbacks.

9. Invest in Yourself: Your education and skills are valuable assets. Continue to invest in your personal and professional growth to enhance your earning potential.

10. Seek Professional Advice: When needed, consult with financial advisors who can offer personalized guidance tailored to your unique situation.

11. Stay Positive: Stay positive and optimistic about your financial journey. Remember that setbacks are a natural part of the process, and each challenge is an opportunity to learn and grow.

12. Celebrate Milestones: Celebrate each financial milestone, no matter how small. Recognize your achievements and use them as motivation to continue moving forward.

Building a strong foundation for financial freedom is a continuous and rewarding endeavor. As you take charge of your finances, you are investing in yourself and creating a brighter future filled with opportunities and choices. Stay persistent, be mindful of your financial decisions, and believe in your ability to shape your financial destiny. Your dedication and hard work today will pave the way for a lifetime of financial security and independence. Remember, you have the power to achieve your financial goals and unlock the door to a life of freedom and abundance.

By grasping these key concepts and incorporating them into your financial journey, you can develop a strong financial foundation that will lead you to long-term financial freedom and security.

You have the power to take charge of your finances and create a secure future for yourselves. Embrace the journey of financial responsibility with confidence and determination, knowing that every step you take towards financial freedom will be worth it in the long run.

Remember that financial education is a powerful tool that empowers you to make informed decisions about money. Take the time to learn and understand the key concepts of personal finance, and don't be afraid to seek advice and guidance when needed.

Create a budget that aligns with your goals and priorities, and be disciplined in managing your expenses. Small sacrifices today can lead to greater financial freedom tomorrow.

Start saving and investing early, even if it's just a small amount. The magic of compound interest can work wonders over time, turning your savings into a solid foundation for the future.

Face commitment on any loan and debt head-on. By managing them responsibly and making timely payments, you can pave the way for a debt-free future.

Build an emergency fund to protect yourself from unexpected financial challenges. Having a safety net will give you peace of mind and keep you on track towards your goals.

Embrace the mindset of continuous learning and improvement. Seek inspiration from the success stories of others who have achieved financial freedom, and let their journeys motivate you to stay committed to your financial goals.

Remember, financial freedom is not an overnight achievement. It's a journey that requires patience, resilience, and perseverance. Celebrate each milestone, no matter how small, and stay focused on your long-term vision.

You have the potential to shape your financial destiny. Take charge of your finances, be proactive in your financial decisions, and believe in your ability to create a bright and secure financial future for yourselves.

You've got this at your finger tips with this book in your custody.

With determination and hard work, you can achieve financial freedom and open doors to a world of opportunities.

Believe in yourself and your abilities. Take the first step towards financial independence today, and let your future self, thank you for the wise choices you make now.

Best wishes on your journey to financial freedom.

ABOUT THE AUTHOR

Sola Akinola, FCA
President/CEO, AVEKORP RESOURCES
CHIEF COACH, AVEKORP ACADEMY

Academic/Professional Qualifications: FCA, MBA (Distinction),
PGDMS, Dip. CIIN, DDP, B. Agricultural Economics (Second Class Upper)
Education: The Management School London, Alperton House, Bridgewater Road, Alperton, England.
Fellow, Institute of Chartered Accountants of Nigeria.
Faculty of Professional Programmes, University of Ilorin, Ilorin, Nigeria.
Obafemi Awolowo University, Ile-Ife, Osun State, Nigeria.
Core Area of Considerable Experience: Coaching & Mentoring, Strategy, Business Development, Strategic Marketing, Accounting and Auditing, Insurance, Risk Management, Project Management and Business Management.
Experience and Recognition:
Over the past 25 years, I have ventured into key business opportunities in various sectors of the economy including Micro, Small and Medium Enterprises (MSME), Oil and Gas, Financial Services and Agricultural businesses.
I have helped to reposition businesses for growth through the implementation of appropriate process improvement and technology solutions. With global and in-depth cross-industry experience, I provide end-to-end services in business process reengineering, solution design, project management, technology implementation, data integrity services, organizational change management, business support and training.
Key Experiences:
- ✔ Business Management

- ✔ Marketing Research and Development for clients.
- ✔ Research and Development
- ✔ Data Management
- ✔ Project Management
- ✔ Financial Products Development.
- ✔ Strategic Marketing to increase market share.
- ✔ Business Expansion and Growth Strategic Plan.
- ✔ Developing Innovative Strategic Business Plan for new ventures.
- ✔ Developing Micro Insurance Products and Platforms for Business growth.
- ✔ Conducting Training on various lines of Businesses for Human Capital Development.

Key Successes:

- Coordinated and achieved N5 Billion sales revenue within 12 months.
- Engaged in product development with income generation potential in excess of ₦3 Billion in the financial industry.
- Managed E-Business Platform, Retail Channels/Agency Network with over N5 Billion income potentials.
- Have over Thirty (30) Books on topical issues of Personal Leadership, Business Management, Accounting and Finance, Strategy and Operations.
- Launched Ten (10) Businesses in key sectors of the economy: Education, Consulting, Financial Services, and Agricultural Businesses.

www.ingramcontent.com/pod-product-compliance
Lightning Source LLC
Chambersburg PA
CBHW071942210526
45479CB00002B/784